# THE NEW STENCIL BOOK

# THE NEW STENCIL BOOK

## INCLUDES OVER 40 STENCIL MOTIFS TO USE

SIMONE SMART

TEXT BY ROSE EVA     PHOTOGRAPHS BY PIA TRYDE

FIREFLY BOOKS

I would like to dedicate this book
to my daughter Lois Aurora

# A FIREFLY BOOK

Published in Canada in 1999 by

Firefly Books Ltd.

3680 Victoria Park Avenue

Willowdale, Ontario, Canada, M2H 3K1


Published in the United States in 1999 by

Firefly Books (U.S.) Inc.

P.O. Box 1338, Ellicott Station

Buffalo, New York, USA, 14205

Cataloguing in Publication Data

Smart, Simone, 1961-

The new stencil book: includes over 40 stencil motifs to use

Includes index.

ISBN 1-55209-299-2

1. Stencil work. I. Tryde, Pia. II. Title.

TT270.S62 1998    745.7'3    C98-931624-6


The publishers acknowledge the financial support of the Government

of Canada through the Book Publishing Industry Development

Program for our publishing activities.


Printed in China

# CONTENTS

# INTRODUCTION

The versatility of stenciling never ceases to surprise me. A tiny sprig on a ceramic mug or a swirling mosaic floor pattern can be equally effective in transforming their particular space. The challenge is to look at that space and to design an image that will enhance it rather than dominate it.

Try to look around you with an open mind, ignoring any preconceived ideas you might have about stenciling. The days of smothering a room with floral designs are long gone; nowadays the emphasis is on understated designs that are sympathetic to the architectural style of a room.

Think carefully about where you want to place an image for best effect. Designs based on plants and leaves – such as my sweet pea motif on page 23 – can be most effective placed near a window to give a sense of the garden coming into the room. This design is also sympathetic to the surface on which it is painted: I used the tongue-and-groove paneling as a form of trellising to 'support' the rambling design.

Once you have chosen your image, you must then learn to see all its potential. Take the toy zebra pattern on page 83, for example. As a repeating border, this is a charming and appealing design. Once the motif has been greatly enlarged, however, so that just the zebra's stripes form the stencil, the result is a bold, dramatic image for cushions or a throw.

Similarly, be prepared to try the same image, or part of that image, on a different scale. The generously sized pot of vigorously climbing squashes, which almost fills the wall space under a window, might be reduced to a tiny detail with which to decorate a dainty ceramic jug (see pages 24-6). To complete the theme, a much larger detail of the main design has been stenciled on to the door of a wall cabinet, giving the room a coordinated, albeit subtle, look.

Rather than just present you with finished projects, I have explained why I have done what I have done, in the hope that this will help you when the time comes for your own decision-

making. Whether framing a window with a garland of leaves, or frosting a mirror with a fish and seaweed design, I have detailed my thought processes and design decisions so that, in turn, you will be able to analyse your available space and deal with the technical challenges that present themselves.

This book is divided into five chapters: four themed stenciling collections and a technical section. Within each section, specific stenciling motifs are introduced and then adapted to suit different purposes. Every design I have used is illustrated within the relevant project, to be traced and transfered to stenciling card, or provided at the back of the book. Please note that some of these designs will need to be enlarged on a photocopier.

All the items that you need to begin stenciling are both illustrated photographically and fully described. The list may look extensive, but once you have your basic tools – stencil board, craft knife and paint (plus brush if you are

not using spray paint) – you can set to work, and get everything else as and when you need it. Throughout the book I explain the techniques I have used, and suggest useful tips gleaned from my experience. The technical section explains the basic principles, describing everything from adapting a design to creating specialised paint effects. Do take time to read and understand this section before you start stenciling: a few extra minutes spent digesting all the information could save you a lot of time correcting mistakes or sorting out self-inflicted problems.

Start with a simple design to build up your confidence, and keep practising until you are happy with the results. As you become more proficient, you can move on to projects that require more skill and perseverance.

Whether you are a practised stenciler looking for a fresh new approach, or a complete novice, who has never stenciled anything before, I hope that you will find just what you need to inspire you in this book.

# ESSENTIAL EQUIPMENT

What most excites me about stenciling is that you can transform a wall or a piece of fabric in minutes. All you need is a piece of stencil board, a paint brush and a few pots of paint, and you will be able to transform any surface into your own masterpiece. What could be simpler?

# MAKING AND CUTTING TOOLS

OPPOSITE *The materials needed for making and cutting stencils can be found in most art shops or stationers. It is worth investing in the correct equipment, as it will make the task of cutting stencils much easier and will enable you to achieve better results.*

## STENCIL BOARD

*I make my stencils using stencil board, which is manila card treated with linseed oil. It is relatively cheap, durable and easy to cut.*

## ACETATE

*This material is very durable as well as transparent, which makes it the perfect choice for aligning repeat patterns. It is, however, more costly and less forgiving to cut than stencil board.*

## STENCIL PAPER

*This is a thick, transparent tracing paper. It is less durable than the other two options, so if you want to use one of my designs for a repeat pattern, it would be worth transfering the design on to acetate.*

## CRAFT KNIFE

*Use a craft knife for cutting out a stencil. It must be sharp, as blunt blades will rip both stencil board and acetate. A rotating blade craft knife will assist with cutting curves. It is advisable to stock up with extra blades when you purchase your knife. A craft knife can be a dangerous thing, so always take great care when cutting stencils.*

## HEAT PEN

*This tool, which looks alarmingly like a dentist's probe, can be used to cut out acetate stencils, making the cutting of this material easier. However, some heat pens can give an unsatisfactory blurred edge to the stencil. They can also be dangerous, so follow the manufacturer's instructions carefully.*

## CUTTING BOARD

*Always use a cutting board to protect your work surface when you are using a craft knife. 'Self-healing' cutting mats, which will last forever, are the best, but a sheet of composite board or even a chopping board will do just as well.*

## GLASS SHEET OR TILE

*Use a glass sheet or tile to protect your work surface when cutting with a heat pen. A cutting board will not withstand the heat.*

## CARBON PAPER

*Good old-fashioned carbon paper is vital for transfering a design on to your stencil.*

## PENCILS AND PENS

*Use pencils for tracing designs and making registration marks; colored crayons or ballpoint pens when transfering a design through carbon paper; and a permanent pen for marking the stencil on stencil card or acetate.*

## SPRAY ADHESIVE

*This non-permanent fixative is used for sticking a stencil on to the surface to be painted. A stencil sprayed with fixative can be repositioned two or three times before it has to be resprayed. It is better to spray a couple of lighter coats than one heavy coat; in this way you can avoid glue patches on your stencil or, worse, traces of glue on the stenciled surface. If you do need to remove these, use a petrol-based cleaner.*

## MASKING TAPE

*Use this for extra security when positioning your stencil, and for mending*

### SAFETY

It is vital to wear a protective face mask when using spray paints or adhesive, as the fumes can be noxious. If you are pregnant, take extra care.

# PAINTING TOOLS

OPPOSITE *There is a wide variety of painting tools that can be used when stenciling. I favor using spray paints – for ease and speed – but you can use stencil brushes and paints, or experiment with other tools to create different decorative effects.*

### SPRAY PAINT

*Spray paints can be bought from car accessory shops and are easy to use. Always read the manufacturer's instructions before spraying, particularly if you are pregnant, and use a face mask (see page 10).*

### BAFFLE

*A baffle is a piece of stencil board or cardboard, folded into a V-shape for easy handling, which is used for deflecting, thereby softening a jet of spray paint, or for protecting parts of a stencil from the jet.*

### STENCIL PAINTS

*These are usually water-based acrylic paints that are applied with a brush or sponge. They dry very quickly. Oil paints dry much more slowly.*

### STENCIL CRAYONS

*These solid blocks of paint produce a soft color when used. You can use stencil crayons in place of paints.*

### CERAMIC PAINTS

*Available both in tubes and in powder form, ceramic paints are used for painting ceramic tiles and pots. Most ceramic paints need to be fixed by baking them in a kiln. Care must be taken when using them because they contain lead. New lead-free varieties are being developed, however.*

### FABRIC PAINTS

*These paints work best on natural fabrics such as cotton and silk. Once applied, the paint needs to be fixed, before the fabric can be laundered – usually by ironing, but sometimes by steaming. Always check the manufacturer's instructions before use.*

### STENCIL BRUSHES

*These round, stubby brushes with blunt ends come in various sizes and are used for transfering color from stencil paints or crayons on to your design. Badger bristle brushes are considered the best, and are the most expensive, but they can be too firm: stencil brushes (which are used dry) need to have a certain amount of 'give' or 'spring.'*

### COLOR SHAPER

*Similar to a paintbrush, but with a shaped rubber tip instead of bristles, a color shaper can be used with ceramic paints.*

### NETTING

*Place netting beneath a stencil to achieve a mottled effect when the paint is applied.*

### SPONGES

*Apply paint with sponges to create a pitted effect.*

### SMALL PAINT ROLLER

*Use a paint roller to apply paint for a smooth effect with no brushmarks.*

### METAL LEAF

*Metal leaf, in different finishes, is used for gilding. Gold size provides the adhesive surface.*

### FROSTING VARNISH

*Stencil this on to glass and mirrors to create a frosted effect.*

### ARTIST'S FIXATIVE

*This fixes paint on surfaces, and prevents it from being rubbed off.*

### CELLULOSE THINNERS

*Dab this on wet spray paint with a cotton swab to correct mistakes.*

### UNIVERSAL MEDIUM

*This creamy liquid can be mixed with ceramic powder paints instead of water. It makes the paint more stable and gives it a good color when fired.*

### SPIRIT LEVEL

*This is used to establish the horizontal on any surface to be decorated. A plumbline, on the other hand, establishes the vertical. Many hardware shops sell a cheap gadget that is a plumbline, spirit level and device for finding a 45 degree angle all in one.*

# THE KITCHEN GARDEN

The house where I grew up had a wonderful kitchen garden. As well as growing cabbages and carrots, we had a big fruit cage, where we grew exotic plants like Chinese gooseberries. The simple shapes of fruit and vegetables and rustic potting-shed tools are the inspirations for my designs.

# THE VEGETABLE TRUG

I have always had a love of vegetables. As a young girl I was often taken to the Chelsea Flower Show in London, where I was fascinated, above all, by the vegetable displays – sumptuous pyramids and baskets piled almost to excess with delicious-looking produce. Although not so ornate, the stands of fresh vegetables at my local market look equally inspiring. I find that the distinctive shapes of cabbages, leeks, squashes and other vegetables lend themselves well to stencil motifs.

I rather like the food connection that can be made using these vegetable motifs - images of

delicious things to eat decorating the dishes from which they are eaten. You can decorate each item with a different vegetable, or use a particularly appropriate vegetable motif for each type of plate or bowl: a tomato on a mug for tomato soup (on one side only, for greater effect), or a carrot or radish on the outside of a salad bowl, for instance.

Of course, the theme can be extended beyond the china to the tablecloth and napkins – for a really coordinated look. I used pure linen with an open weave for my stenciled tablecloth, shown here, but voile or muslin would do just as well. Cheap cloth napkins can then be decorated with a scaled-down matching motif in one corner.

## USING SPACE IN DESIGN

It can be tempting to over-use a stencil and decorate the whole of the available surface with repeating motifs. However, single motifs can look more effective, as on this tablcloth, where I stenciled one almost full-sized leek in each corner rather than creating a border of leeks. Restraint is vital in stenciling, because the background – whether it be a rough brick wall or a pure linen tablecloth – is just as important as the image itself. A single, judiciously placed motif creates much more of an impact than a surface smothered in decoration; it is the difference between stylish simplicity and fussiness.

The size of the design is also important. I suggest keeping vegetable stencils more or less life-size; one full-sized pea pod on a salad bowl

RIGHT *I designed this stencil of a laden vegetable trug (flat basket) to fit this wooden tray, but you could achieve an equally impressive effect by using the stencil for the trug (see page 121) and then filling it with the vegetable stencils on these pages.*

*• A plain wooden tray needs a couple of coats of latex paint before being stenciled, to provide an evenly colored surface. Once your design has been sprayed in place, use three coats of acrylic varnish to seal it.*

is much more dramatic than lots of little ones arranged in a pattern. It is therefore important to think about the space to be decorated before starting work, and to decide which motif works best in each location.

## STENCILING ON TO ENAMEL

Enamel plates, bowls and mugs – the sorts of things you can buy from camping shops – are excellent items on which to practise stenciling: they are inexpensive; any slight chips that they accumulate add to their charm; and, more importantly, as paints dry relatively slowly on enamel, any mistakes can be wiped off. These stenciled plates and mugs make great picnic ware, for while being rugged and virtually indestructible, they are attractive enough to use for an alfresco party.

You can now buy special paints for ceramics and metal which are very effective for use with stencils. These water-based paints come in a wide range of bright colors. The manufacturer recommends that food should not come into direct contact with this paint, so it is wise to plan

your work so that the stencils appear on the outside of mugs and bowls, or are used on items that have a purely decorative purpose.

To stencil on enamel, first gently rub the area to be stenciled with steel wool to 'key' the surface so that the paint can adhere. Position the stencil by eye rather than by careful measuring with a ruler, as slight differences in a set add a certain casual charm, then stipple on the special paint. Once your design is dry, bake it in the oven to make it dishwasher-proof (following the manufacturer's instructions).

# SWEET PEAS AND PODS

Sweet peas are one of the few flowers that are equally at home in both the kitchen garden and the flower garden. I have sweet peas in my garden, and although I do very little to look after them, they still grow and blossom year after year, producing their seed-filled pods as the summer ends. The flower heads may be any one of a wide range of pastel colors, even on one plant, which is why sweet pea motifs look so effective when stenciled in mixed colors.

Sweet peas are fragile-looking flowers, making them highly suitable for stencil motifs with light applications of paint: the lighter the touch, the better. The wide color variations in the flowers mean that they lend themselves to almost any color scheme, making them endlessly adaptable.

## STENCILING ON TO PANELING

Sweet peas look lovely stenciled on to tongue-and-groove paneling; the alternating panels and recesses form a framework over which the flowers can ramble, as they do in nature. Despite the uneven surface of the paneling, careful positioning of the stencil and lightly sprayed paint give excellent results.

To produce a naturalistic-looking stencil, I lined up the tendrils to produce the effect that they are clinging on to the grooves for support, as they would to trellising, while allowing the flowers to roam across the surface. If you are adapting this stencil to fit paneling of a different width to mine, try to make sure the larger areas of color do not fall in the grooves. If necessary, move the stencil a little as you work, to keep the design on the paneling rather than in the gaps between. Make sure that the stencil is well stuck down, and spray merely a hint of color into the grooves, to prevent the paint seeping.

I wanted to keep the freshness and crisp, clean look of the paneling, and not detract from it with too much color, so rather than sprinkling them around the room, I stenciled the sweet peas only under the window. This avoided the potentially overpowering and fussy effect of too many flower motifs in the

RIGHT *A small area of the sweet pea design – a flower and a curling tendril – has been stenciled on to a pyjama pocket with fabric paint for a pretty decoration.*
*• Keep on hand a pot of paint the same color as your background, to touch up any mistakes or areas where the paint has seeped under the stencil. Alas, this is not possible with fabric – any mistakes are there for keeps.*

room, and also created an illusion of delicate, summery flowers growing naturally in through the window.

## STENCILING ON TO FABRIC

One way to continue the sweet pea theme throughout the room, without overdoing it on the walls, is to stencil the motif on to soft furnishings or on to items of clothing, such as the pocket of a pair of pyjamas, or the corner of a bed throw or cushion. You will need to use paint specially formulated for fabric, and always check the manufacturer's instructions.

Pick out an area of the design that you like, such as one flower and a tendril, and mask out the rest, or re-cut the stencil if you prefer. Iron the fabric flat. Stick the stencil in place with spray adhesive, and then, to ensure a really crisp image, turn the fabric over and work it gently into the windows of the stencil with your fingers. Take special care with the thin sections, such as the tendrils.

Fabric paint is applied in the same manner as stencil paint, but, as fabric is more absorbent than most surfaces, you will need to use more paint. You can, however, dilute it with an extender to make it go further. Be careful when painting on fabric: once the paint is on, it cannot be removed. Make sure the fabric is of single thickness and not folded or paint will seep through to the underlying layers. It is best to place some newspaper underneath, or, if you are decorating a pocket, slip a piece of stencil board into the pocket to protect the fabric behind.

Dip the brush lightly into the paint and work off the excess on a cloth before dabbing at the stencil. For a stronger effect, use two light coats of paint rather than one thicker one.

# CLIMBING SQUASHES

I used to grow squashes and ornamental gourds. They grew rapidly, wrapping their lovely long tendrils around the other plants and taking over the entire vegetable patch. Now you can find them in supermarkets, with such splendid names as Turk's Turban and Happy Jack. With their wonderful bulbous shapes and splendid colors, squashes make interesting stencil motifs.

## LOOKING AT THE SPACE

Choosing the right image and, just as importantly, the right scale for that image is absolutely vital when looking at the room you are going to decorate. So, before you begin stenciling, look at your space and find an image that pleases you and is the right scale to suit the room. The image should not dominate the room but, conversely, it should not be overwhelmed by it.

The room I chose for this stencil was big, bright and sunny, with windows looking out on to a garden at a higher level than the room itself, making it feel as if the garden was creeping into the room. A delicate, conventionally pretty design such as sweet peas would have been completely inappropriate for the room's bright, robust feel. I needed something large, so I decided to stencil squashes – huge, great, colorful fruit that did not look too tiny in the large space and which allowed the garden outside to enter the room but not dominate it.

Rather than have the squashes wandering freely around the room, I decided to anchor them – and the design – with a large stenciled pot, which created a pleasing focal point. While the effect is not intended to be trompe l'oeil, the pot provides a delightful visual echo of the plant-holder on the window sill (see page 29).

## VARYING YOUR DESIGN

If I had stenciled the squashes in my design without any variation, the result might have been a little monotonous, but I did not want to design a whole new stencil to avoid that effect. I found that by angling the stencil and masking out, I was able to achieve a completely different look to the squash design as it curled to right and left of the pot and I had to cut out only one new piece of stem. The pot was the only thing for which I measured up, as I placed it carefully under the window, opposite the door.

## PAINTING ON TO CERAMICS

Although the squash design is enormous, it can look very effective brought into a small corner of the room, on a completely different scale. I painted a tiny orange squash on to a white ceramic cream jug, which now lives in a corner cabinet, on which I had painted a smaller version of the whole design.

*OPPOSITE Here a tiny, orange squash motif has been stenciled on to a ceramic cream jug using ready-mixed ceramic paint. Once it has been fired in a kiln, the design will be dishwasher-proof.*
*• Take into account the background color of the room you are decorating. I painted the walls a soft grey-green, both to give a mellow effect and to link the room with the garden outside.*

THIS PAGE *The original stencil was several times bigger than the one shown here, and big enough to satisfy any child on Hallowe'en night. Do not be put off by a large stencil such as this: although it might seem a little daunting at first sight, with its curling tendrils and segmented squashes, it is easier to cut than smaller, more complicated designs. It does help to use stencil board or paper rather than acetate for an intricate design such as this. Once it is cut, it can be used repeatedly at different angles to achieve a very impressive effect. To create variety in the design, the squashes to the right and left of the pot were placed at different angles; the extra bit of stem that I added completes the effect, so that the squashes appear to have grown out of the pot and across the room.*

Plain white- or cream-glazed objects, such as tiles or bone china mugs, make suitable surfaces for ceramic paint stenciling. Do not stencil onto colored objects, because the refiring process necessary to fix the ceramic paint can alter colored glazes significantly. Microwave-proof ceramics are not really suitable for stenciling.

Ceramic paints normally come in two forms, as powder paint and ready-mixed in tubes. For beginners, I recommend the ready-mixed paints because they are generally easier to get to grips with. Squeeze a blob of paint on to a spare tile or palette, add a drop of water and mix it with a spoon to the consistency of peanut butter. If you do use powder paints, put some powder on a tile, add some universal medium (see page 12) and mix to the same consistency. You can, if you wish, use water instead of universal medium, but the paint will be less stable.

When using ceramic paints, make sure that you have only a tiny amount of paint on your

brush. Keep the brush upright, and dab rather than stroke the paint on to the stencil. Because the color tends to slide around somewhat on a glazed surface, you will find that if you use your brush on its side, you can literally push the paint away, resulting in a smeared image. You must work with a very light touch, especially when shading, because if you are heavy-handed, you might remove the first layer of paint.

Keep a steady hand when decorating curved surfaces such as jugs and mugs; it is all too easy to let your hand slip. Do not panic, however, should an error occur. Even though it dries quickly, ceramic paint can be removed right up to the moment it is fired, so if you make a mistake you can simply wipe off the offending paint and start again. This makes it much easier to work on ceramics than fabric, where mistakes are almost impossible to remove. When you have finished painting, rinse your brush in water.

A color shaper (a paintbrush with a tapered, rubber-tipped point) is absolutely invaluable for correcting or altering a design on a ceramic surface; you can use it just like a finger nail to remove tiny areas of misplaced paint.

Ceramic paint must be fired in a kiln to cure it, following the manufacturer's instructions. (Contact your local education center, who may be able to advise you about using a kiln at a local pottery class.) Do not be dismayed if your designs, once painted in place and dry, look rather dull before they are fired: they will be noticeably brighter by the time they come out of the kiln. They will also be heat-durable and dishwasher-proof.

For instructions on how to use some new ceramic paints that come in pots and which can be baked in a home oven, see page 19.

LEFT *While the stenciled pot has been positioned centrally beneath the window, the squashes appear to be growing organically across the wall. By turning and twisting the stencil, you can create your own design.*

*• Do not be afraid of obscuring parts of your decoration with other objects; set against the wall, furniture, such as tables, can enhance the effect, with your stencil peeping out from behind and underneath. After all, it is rare to see things in nature completely unobscured.*

# GARDENING TOOLS

My father used to collect old tools, and when I was young we had whole chests full of them. The shapes of old-fashioned garden tools are lovely: clean, simple and rustic, and often much more attractive than their streamlined modern-day successors. With my stenciled potting-shed tool motifs, I have tried to capture a bygone era, one before chemical fertilizers and mechanical cultivation methods ruled the day.

## STENCILING ON TO DIFFERENT SURFACES

To stencil on to objects with curved sides, such as a bucket or pot, you will need to render a new or relatively unused stencil fairly flexible, so that it fits snugly around these shapes. To do this, roll the stencil gently into a tube shape. Make sure you just roll, rather than folding it, because a stencil folded with a crease will be ruined. Once a stencil has been rolled, it does seem to retain its flexibility, which makes it suitable for bending around curved surfaces. (Please note: this does not work on older stencils, because the residue of paint that will have accrued is likely to crack and cause the stencil itself to crack.)

When you are cutting a stencil for a tiny object, make sure the stencil board is no larger than the item to be stenciled, otherwise the painting process can be a bit difficult to handle. A similar rule applies when making a stencil for an area that has a raised surface around it. If the stencil is too big, it will be raised off the surface by the embossed design or ridge, and, as a result, the paint will spread under the stencil and the image will be blurred. A small stencil that fits

within these raised areas, however, will rest flat against the surface and so produce a crisp image.

Stick the stencil to the surface using spray adhesive, and add a few strips of masking tape around the edges of your stencil board for extra security. Masking tape is also useful for securing your designs to uneven surfaces, such as brick-work, where spray adhesive alone might not be sufficient. If you are working outside, try to avoid damp, windy days, because nothing will stick to wet bricks.

When stenciling on to a moderately dark surface, such as brickwork, put your stencil in place and give it a quick spray with grey primer before applying your chosen color(s). This blocks out the background color, and also seals the surface, so that the colors of the design do not seep into the bricks and so lose their resonance. If the surface to be decorated is darker still – such as the wood of my beach hut (see page 49) – you will need to use white primer.

## THREE-DIMENSIONAL DESIGNS

Large designs, such as a full-sized watering can or garden spade, can look a little uninspiring if painted in the same tone throughout. To give your design interest and variety, try to vary your paint application to give the impression of shading. If you can make the edges of the stencil appear darker than the center, then your design will look more three-dimensional. To do this, spray the color gently around the edges of your stencil to build up the shading; because of the diffuse way in which the spray comes out of the

ABOVE *The graphic lines of this rustic dibber, with its flowing curves of string, make a perfect subject for a stencil. Use fabric paint to stencil this design on to what would otherwise be an ordinary pair of gardening gloves.*

OPPOSITE *I chose earthy shades of brown and green for these tool motifs (see page 123), and applied the paint without too much finesse, for a rustic appearance.*

can, you will lightly fill the middle of the design with color even if you do not actually paint there. You can strengthen the effect by adding touches of a darker color around the edge; for example, some olive green shading over a paler lime green.

Extra detailing can also add to the three-dimensional effect. To give a little more detail on the watering can, I retained the sprinkler nozzle piece of the stencil, and cut tiny holes in it. Once I had sprayed the whole stencil in a light color, I then repositioned the sprinkler piece and resprayed this area in a darker shade. The resulting darker dots on the watering can's nozzle make the image more eye-catching. In the same way, a completely different color, such as a bit of brown at the bottom of a spade to suggest mud, can also add authenticity to the effect.

I used spray paints to decorate these new aluminum buckets with gardening motifs. Just three basic colors – an olive green, a dark spruce green and a brown – will be sufficient to begin with. In fact, you can create most of the garden motifs we have provided with these colors. Spray paint is incredibly hard-wearing (it was developed for use on cars, after all) and will last outside in the elements for ages, so do not worry about leaving your pots outside.

It is easy to work on new aluminum: just bend your new stencil gently and attach it with spray adhesive and some masking tape, then spray on your design. If you go incredibly wrong with your stenciling, you can use cellulose thinners to wipe away the paint without damaging the metal. If the spray adhesive leaves a residue on the bucket, wash it off with soap and water once the paint is dry.

If you are looking for gifts for green-thumbed friends and members of your family, you cannot go wrong with stenciled gardener's gloves and aprons. They are not washed too often, so spray paints are quite suitable.

ABOVE *These stenciled garden tools (see stencils on page 119) add a touch of trompe l'oeil to a plain wall.*

LEFT *A pair of snipping shears and some tumbling leaves can transform an aluminum bucket in minutes.*

# AT THE
# SEASIDE

The seaside provides
constant inspiration for
my designs. Images of
foam-flecked waves, fish
and shells in all shapes and
sizes, tendrils of seaweed,
and stylish sailing boats can
be used to create a variety
of stencils. You can use
seaside motifs to decorate
children's rooms, bathrooms
and even clothing.

# SEAWEED, BUBBLES AND FISH

I love the stylized Roman wave pattern that you see on ancient urns. Reproducing that pattern in frothy bubbles makes the design more contemporary and humorous. Fish, too, make lovely decorative images. You can stencil individual fish or a whole group swimming along a surface.

## CURVED SURFACES

To stencil on to curved surfaces requires a different technique from that used when working on flat surfaces, as placing and securing the stencil can be tricky. Stenciling bubbles on to a freestanding, roll-top bath meant that the design had to curve around the bath. So I chose a very simple motif that was suitable for the clean shape of the bath, and was fairly easy to stencil.

On large, rounded surfaces, careful measuring can be difficult. To overcome this, measure a set distance from the floor and make a few marks in pencil on the surface, then position your stencil by eye. An informal, flowing pattern, such as these bubbles, allows you to be flexible in positioning, and to adjust the design to fit.

To enable the stencil to lie flush against the curved surface, make small cuts into the edges of the board. Overlap the cut sections very slightly to allow the stencil to bend around the curve, and secure it with masking tape, covering the cuts at the same time. To make the repeating pattern, place the first bubble hole of the new repeat over the last bubble of the old, then move the board forward by half an inch.

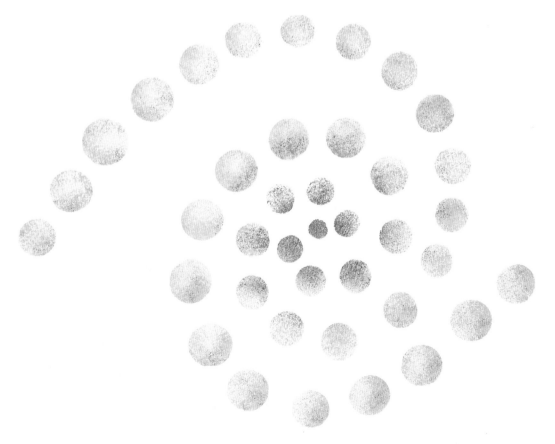

RIGHT *Achieving colored
frosting is very simple,
and is a particularly
effective look when used
on mirror-glass. Clean
the working surface
thoroughly, as before.
Attach the fish and
seaweed stencil (see
page 123) with spray
adhesive and then cover
the surrounding area with
paper to protect it. Stencil
a first layer in colored
acrylic spray paint (I used
dark blue). Leave this to
dry for a minute or two.
Without removing the
stencil, stipple on a
second layer – this time
of white frosting varnish.
Stippling produces an
attractive textured
finish. Remove the
stencil very carefully
and leave for 24 hours.
Excess paint or varnish
can be removed with
mineral spirits.*

LEFT *Adapting the seaweed and bubbles motif (see page 123) for a border is more straightforward than it appears. There is some tricky cutting out initially, but once you have cut out the template, all the hard work is done: start cutting out the stencil in the areas where the 'windows' are closest together. As two colors are used for this design, a masking stencil is essential (see page 44). The repeatable stencil takes in a single corner and two of the bubble waves, but you will still need to follow the instructions for handling corners described on page 111.*

## STENCILING ON TO VINYL

Transparent plastic shower curtains can be glamorized with the addition of stenciled motifs, such as these gleaming white fish. To save on painting time, cut a stencil of three fish, rather than just one. Secure the stencil to the curtain with spray adhesive, then spray your design. The adhesive will leave a sticky residue on the surface, but if you leave the design to dry overnight, you can wash it off easily.

## CUTTING CIRCLES

Circular shapes, such as the bubbles in the seaweed and bubbles design, need to be cut out using a special method. To cut out circles in stencil card, you must first cut half of the shape and then, turn the stencil card around (see pages 104–105) to cut out the other half. In this way, your beveling angle will remain correct. With an abstract pattern, you do not need to be exact with your cutting lines, as any imperfections will simply add interest to the design.

## FROSTED EFFECTS

Etching on glass is a specialized and expensive business, but you can achieve a similar effect at home using frosting varnish: a white acrylic varnish, the consistency of heavy cream, which is stippled on to clean, dry glass. The glass should be at room temperature. You can use a stencil brush for a consistent texture, but I prefer to use a child's paintbrush, as the rough bristles give a more interesting effect. Alternatively, you can use a sponge for a mottled texture. The frosting varnish must be left to dry overnight.

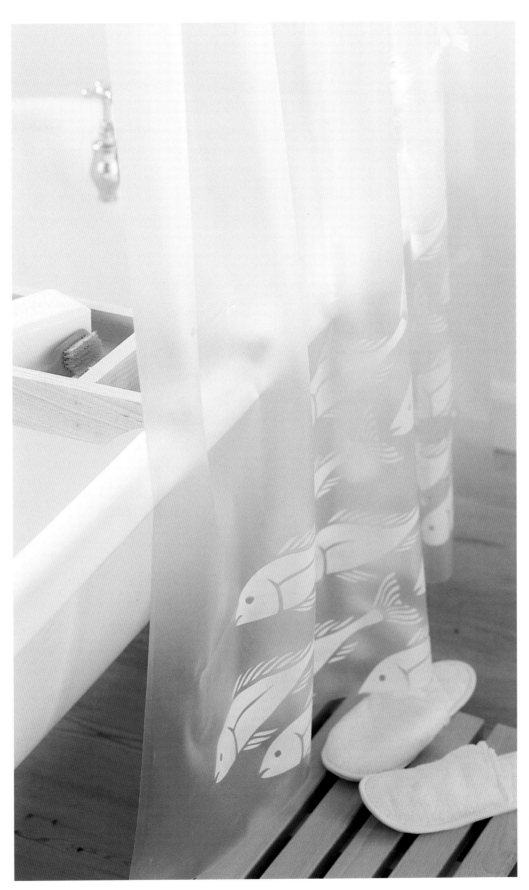

LEFT *Spray paints are really the only paints durable enough for use on shower curtains. This fishy design is one of the easiest to achieve, but do not forget to put in the eyes of the fish every time you paint the stencil. Careful measuring and placing is not essential in this design; the motif can be repeated randomly over the surface, rather as a school of fish might swim in water.*

# SAILING BOATS AND BUNTING

OPPOSITE *Masking stencils allow you to mix and match colors, an effect that worked well with these sailing boats.*

BELOW *Adapting the design by reducing its size and using just one color provides an equally effective image.*

I went to the seaside on a wintry day when there was not another soul on the beach. The weather was stormy and the waves were crashing. I found the foaming water, the patterns of the seaweed on the sand, and the bright beach huts against the steely sky, immensely inspiring.

I wanted to decorate the walls of the hut so that it would look lively even out of season. The sailing boat stencil I came up with would also suit a bathroom or children's bedroom.

Before you mark your positional grid, it might be useful to spray six rough copies of the stencil onto paper, cut them out, and stick them lightly in place to check for spacing and height. When

you are satisfied with the position of the boats, mark your grid of two horizontal and three vertical lines, noting that the six points where the lines cross indicate the positions for the center of the stencil. To position your stencil correctly, use the grid lines to align the boat with the stencil board each time.

## COLOR PLANNING

I chose to paint the boats in two rows for this design. I wanted each of them to have sails and decks in different color combinations. As the area surrounding the stencil needs covering with protective paper at each stenciling, it is essential to draw a plan on a piece of paper before you start, indicating where the colors you are using are to fall.

## MASKING STENCILS

Using a masking stencil is the simplest way of spraying stencils in more than one color. You certainly need to make one for this design. Spray the stencil on to a second piece of stencil board, then draw a line around each of the color areas (see full instructions on page 108–109). Here, I cut five masking stencils, one for each of the color areas (the deck-top and mast, the hull, the main-sail, the foresail and the pennant). In addition, I cut an extra masking stencil combining the deck-top, the mast and the pennant (see boat bottom left). You can re-use the masking stencils as you re-spray the design in different colors. The spray paint should be dry on the board by the time you have repositioned the stencil and thus protected the surrounding area.

## BUNTING

Flags and pennants dot a shoreline of boats and dinghies, but they can also be seen away from nautical circles. During local festivities, brightly colored bunting is often strung across the streets. I used this motif to decorate the exterior of the beach hut, but you could also use this design in children's bedrooms and playrooms.

## STENCILING ON TO DUTCH PANELING

The exterior of the beach hut is made of Dutch paneling which, although similar to tongue-and-groove, has a different surface. It consists of alternating panels of timber, one above the surface, one recessed, the recessed areas being wide and deep. Tongue-and-groove comprises a series of panels with narrow recessed areas, or grooves, between them. Although perfectly acceptable on tongue-and-groove, the technique of spraying lightly into the grooves does not work on Dutch paneling.

If you have to contend with recesses, lightly mark the areas where the flags will be in pencil,

and stick masking tape along these lines on the recessed panels before you fix the stencil in position with spray adhesive. Then, when you paint the stencil, the image should remain crisp and bright, even in the recesses. Any smudged lines can be cleaned up with cellulose thinners and a cotton swab.

With spray paints, it is vital that you know which color paint is in each can. Unfortunately, the color is marked only on the lid, so once it is off, you will have no idea what color is in the can. To prevent disaster, write the color on a piece of tape, and stick it on to the body of the can.

## STENCILING ON TO DARK AREAS

When stenciling on to dark-colored paneling, bright colors will change in tone and become muted. To keep the effect bright, put the stencil in place, and give it a quick spray with white primer before spraying on your chosen colors, while leaving the rope white. I did this on the wall of the hut, and the colors stand out beautifully against the dark blue background.

OPPOSITE *My flag templates end with a small twist of rope. You can change the twists and pieces in your design to add variety and make the bunting more realistic, and, of course, to make the design fit any space.*

*• If you reduce a design significantly, it is often wise to simplify it; when I painted little flags on my deckchairs, I gave them plain rope tails.*

OPPOSITE *It was a simple matter to paint these flags on the canvas of the deckchairs. I did the stenciling in situ, then laid the canvas on the ironing board and ironed both back and front to fix the colors.*

LEFT *A beach hut is exposed to all the elements, particularly wind and sea spray, and unless you want your design to look fashionably distressed, it would be wise to seal it with a few coats of exterior-quality polyurethane varnish.*

# OARS

The seaside theme can easily be extended to fabrics and soft furnishings. I brightened up a beach towel by decorating it with oars, and also made a jaunty canvas beach bag.

## STENCILING ON TO FABRIC

Using fabric paints, I stippled a pair of oars on to two pieces of canvas, which I then stitched to the top and bottom of a large towel. These simple additions transform a plain bath towel into a beach towel of which you can be proud. Make sure that the thread on your sewing machine matches the color of the canvas, and that the thread in the bobbin matches that of the towel; in this way the stitching will not show up on either the towel or the canvas.

The areas of color on the blades of the oars, and the bridges separating them, are both rather narrow, so it is worth masking out the surrounding areas with tape even when you use a stencil brush, to avoid mixing the colors on the design.

This canvas bag is a simple construction of two squares of canvas stitched together (with a turnover to the inside at the top for a facing), and two sturdy cord handles. Use an eyelet kit to make strong holes for the handles. The head-to-tail oar design is simple, but the colors make the bag an instant success.

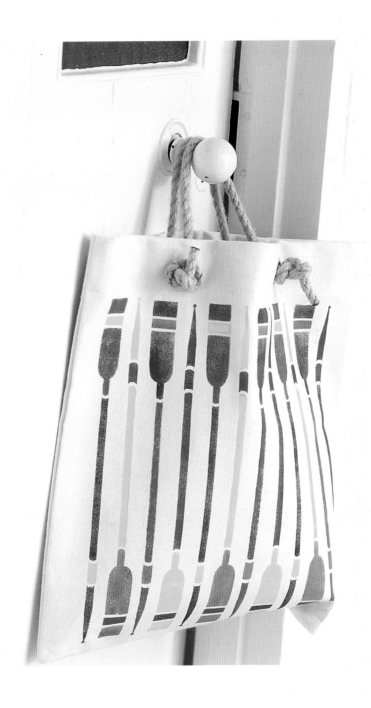

# THE
# COUNTRY
# PARK

Many of my stencils are
inspired by my love of nature,
and the changing colors
of the different seasons can
be echoed in stencil designs.
A single leaf motif painted
in a summery fresh green
can be given an autumnal
feel with just a touch of
golden brown. The leaf and
urn designs, formal topiary
and heraldic statuary
shown in this chapter are
all great fun to paint.

# TOPIARY AND PLANTERS

I once went to a wedding in France, which was held at a château near La Rochelle. The gardens were very formal and divided into distinct areas, almost like horticultural rooms. Some were divided by yew hedges cut into topiary shapes, while others contained obelisks and statuary, artfully placed. These elegant forms are perfect for creating grand effects in stencil design.

A few years ago I watched someone making the wire armatures around which topiary plants grow. The shapes were lovely – balls and poles alongside more exotic shapes, such as birds and even teddy bears – and as stencils they can be adapted to suit almost any location. Used life-sized, they can frame a door and give a touch of grandeur to a room, but they can look equally chic used in miniature on a cushion cover.

## MEASURING THE SPACE

Unlike the relaxed look of the kitchen garden motifs, where stencils can be positioned by eye, formal designs like topiary and planters need precise placing. I wanted to stencil the designs above the kitchen sink, but there were various constraints, such as the kitchen tap and the cupboards above, below and at either side. Accurate positioning was vital. In fact, the most challenging part of this job was the measuring.

OPPOSITE *Protect all your surfaces when you are working, especially when you are stenciling in a tight space. When decorating this small alcove above the kitchen sink, I covered every available surface with drop cloths to prevent stray spray paint from ruining the adjoining areas.*

Always measure the space to be stenciled accurately, then check that the stencil design will fit the setting and is an appropriate size; if necessary, you can enlarge or reduce the image on a photocopier until it is a suitable size. Mark the vertical line clearly on your stencil. Using a soft pencil, make a mark on the surface where you want each stencil to be centered; you can remove the dot later with an artist's kneaded rubber or a good-quality eraser. Align the vertical line on the stencil with the marked dot and make sure the line is upright. For smaller surfaces, use a set square to make sure this line is vertical. For large areas, a spirit level will give you a true vertical. If you spend time getting the measuring right, you will not be faced with the lengthy job of painting out mistakes and starting again.

## CHOOSING COLORS

Before you start spraying your chosen surface, experiment with different colors for your design. Spray the stencil design in different colors on

to heavy paper, then cut them out and place them on the surface to be decorated to see what looks best.

My original choice of naturalistic greens and browns looked too quaint when I tested them in the kitchen, so I then tried the image in solid black. When your colors are not working, a black silhouette is always a good starting point. It may not be the right color for the design, but working with a single block of color can indicate in which direction to proceed. Although I liked the effect that black produced, it was too stark for the kitchen, so I ended up spraying the design lightly in grey and black, which looked very smart.

Colors that work in one location may not be suitable for another. While green and brown looked wrong in the stylish kitchen, they looked perfect on the single images I used on the garden bench cushions, and on the smaller, solid topiary shapes that I stenciled along the long seat cushion (see stencil on page 123).

OPPOSITE *When stenciling cushions like these, extensive masking out is not necessary. On the larger images, I simply masked the relevant area with a piece of paper, while on the small designs I used a baffle. This allowed for some blending of the colors, lending softness to otherwise hard images.*

RIGHT *These linking devices can be used effectively between individual images in a row of topiary planters to create a border design.*

# LEAF DESIGNS

The humble leaf may not be a treasured object, but it has a certain dignity, a fact not lost on the ancient Romans, who crowned their emperors with laurel leaves, not jewels. Leaf shapes have an unfussy elegance about them, making them ideal subjects for continuous stenciled patterns.

## FRAMING A WINDOW

Round windows are notoriously difficult to hang curtains around, so if they are not overlooked, you might dispense with curtains altogether. However, without curtains or a sill, a round window can be lost in the wall. A little stenciled decoration around the window can provide definition, anchoring the window in the room.

There is some beautiful ivy just outside my round window, so I decided to echo this lovely greenery inside the room. The round shape of the window is so attractive, however, that I did not want to detract from it with a specific leaf

OPPOSITE *The long, graceful leaves of the design echo the shape of the window, but do not follow its curves exactly. With judicious placing and masking out, this simple repeat design could be adapted to frame a standard square window. It could also be painted above a window in place of curtains.*

RIGHT *This simple border design transforms a plain coir mat into a decorative feature. The leaf stencil is very flexible, and you could add further variety by placing alternate motifs in opposite directions. It is vital to fix the fabric paints by ironing them; otherwise the colors will fade very quickly.*

LEFT *To make a
neat finish to the
border, with no loss of
design, you will need
to miter the corners.
Where the border strips
overlap, fold back the
excess fabric to create
a diagonal line on each
corner. Then slipstitch
the strips together along
both the front and the
back diagonal seams.
Repeat at each corner.*

design, such as oak or ivy leaves. Instead I used a stylized leaf design with a wispy knot to finish off the center (see page 119). You can paint this leaf shape using any colors you like, because the design is not meant to reflect any particular leaf. I used an autumnal rust tone tinged with green, which complemented a pair of Chinese lacquer chests, painted in emperor red and black, that live in the room. You might prefer to use an apple green tinged with yellow to create a summery feel, or a rich, dark green flecked with white for a more dramatic look.

## CREATING BORDERS

A decorative stenciled border stitched around a plain coir floor mat (see pages 62–3) can give an otherwise plain and uninteresting mat a more stylish finish. To make the stenciled border, first measure the length and width of the mat. Then cut two strips of fabric (I used linen, but you could use canvas) 4 inches longer than the mat itself, and two strips the same width as the mat plus 4 inches. All four strips should be about 12 inches wide, although if your mat is much smaller than mine, it might be wise to opt for slightly narrower strips. Turn under both long edges of each strip and iron them to make the strips straight and neat.

Stencil the border design (see page 119) on the 'right' side of all four strips using fabric paints, then leave them to dry. Iron the strips, following the manufacturer's instructions, to 'fix' the colors so that they do not fade. Using strong button thread and a darning needle, stitch the two long borders to the top of the mat, then add the shorter borders, and miter the corners (see page 63). Fold the strips over to the back of the mat, and secure with a strong adhesive.

The leaf design complements the coir mat, maintaining the natural feel of the matting but making it much more stylish. The symmetrical design of leaves around a circle allows the leaves to branch off in opposite directions. It also makes the stencil easier to alter to fit any size.

To add a border to a smaller surface, such as the top of this occasional table, cut out a whole rectangular stencil to fit the surface, and spray it just once. Given the simplicity of the leaf stencil, it is easier to do this than to cut just one leaf and repeat it. When the stencil paint is dry, apply a coat or two of matt acrylic varnish to protect the table and the design.

When I applied this stencil, the old paint on the table reacted with the new spray paint of the design, making it separate slightly to resemble shark skin. Although this detail was not planned as part of the design, it looked very effective, and shows why one needs to have a flexible attitude: unexpected things can happen and strange combinations occur, but the results can be great.

OPPOSITE *Just one large stencil was used to decorate this table, making it a very simple and speedy project.*

BELOW LEFT *The same stencil painted in autumnal colors transforms a simple doormat into a stylish entrance to a house. To paint matting, use a stipple brush and multi-purpose craft paint, and push the paint right to the base of the matting to give both greater depth and durability to the color.*

65

PREVIOUS PAGES
*A miniature urn*
*brightens up the*
*cover of a journal or*
*photograph album.*
*These little stencils*
*were spray painted,*
*because it would have*
*been too difficult*
*to try complicated*
*paint effects on this*
*scale. The leaves*
*were left unstriped*
*but their tips were*
*shaded a light green to*
*emphasize their length.*

# URNS

Big, bulbous pots filled with spiky agave plants are wonderfully evocative of Central and South America. In Mexico, these plants grow to a height of 10 feet or more. Their dramatically long, fleshy leaves, with dangerously serrated edges, form captivating patterns in the hot landscape.

Although spray paints are suitable for most stenciling, being easy to use, quick to dry and marvelous for blending colors, they have their limitations. To achieve the effects I wanted for this design, I had to employ other techniques (see pages 112-13 for details).

For the agave plant design, I wanted to achieve an almost 'scratchy' look, in keeping with the spiky, variegated leaves, so I chose to use artist's acrylic paints and applied them with an old stencil brush. Start with a buff-colored paint, and drag the brush up the leaves. Then repeat this process with a light, bright green, and finally touch in the stencil with a darker green, making sure that the spikes are painted in. This produces a textured, striped effect, with the colors showing alongside each other rather than being blended in smoothly as they would with spray paints. To emphasize the striped quality of the foliage, I kept the stencil bridges separating the leaves to a uniform thickness.

The urn was stenciled using a different method to convey its rounded, hand-thrown finish. To achieve this look, two similar shades of latex paint were used, one darker than the other. The paler color was applied with a sponge, and then dragged in a slight curve across the pot, both to give an impression of the lines in the clay caused by the hand-throwing of the urn, and to produce a three-dimensional effect. Then darker paint was added as shadow to the side of the urn facing away from the window, an effect you can reproduce in your room, so that it appears as if the pot is lit by natural light. On a smaller scale, I used a simplified version of this design to decorate some books (see pages 66-7).

# STATUARY

Every day I pass a pair of large, fierce-looking dogs on a pair of black gates guarding the entrance to Malmesbury House in Salisbury, England. Inspired by these statues, I decided to stencil two enormous hounds to keep watch on either side of my front door.

The space I had available for the dogs was quite narrow, and so the design could project upwards, but not outwards. This meant that the animals had to tuck in quite neatly. Rather than having to compromise on the size of the dogs, I designed their heads with long muzzles, to turn upwards, which added to their heraldic air. The animals were raised on a plinth to bring them to a height that matched the panels on the door. The size of the plinth can be varied, of course, or it can be dispensed with altogether.

While most aerosols, with their slight sheen, are suitable for the majority of stencils, I make a point of using a matt finish for animals, as I think this looks more natural. I used a dusty grey aerosol primer and secured this with fixative, then added a darker charcoal for shadow. I sprayed the collar dark brown and black, to match the wood of the front door. As the body area is so large, it adds interest to spray it in a rather blotchy way, while still maintaining a light touch.

The greyhound stencil could also be used on a firescreen. Enlarge the animal as required, then cut out the design in composite board, leaving an extra half an inch all around as a margin. Paint the board with cream latex, then stencil the dog on top. Make a small wooden foot on which to stand the screen.

OPPOSITE *The dogs make much more of an impact in the room as a pair rather than stenciled as a continuous repeat. I deliberately chose to design stylized dogs, so I left out their tails and eyes, and did not cut many windows in the stencil. If you prefer a sleeping hound to a guard dog, try the stencil on page 119.*

# SIMPLE
# PATTERNS

A stencil design does not
have to be complicated to be
effective. The simpler the
project, the more manageable
it is to achieve, and the
greater the chances are of
getting it right. As in so many
things, less in stenciling
is more. In this chapter,
several simple patterns are
used to create stunning
repeat designs.

# MOROCCAN STAR

In North Africa there is a strong tradition of repetitive design. Simple shapes in bright yet subtle, chalky colors, glowing against the ochers and sienna tones of the Moroccan landscape, are repeated to an almost mesmerizing degree. This glorious combination of colors and shapes was the inspiration for my star stencil.

## CRUMB CLOTHS

In times past, most American households used to place canvas mats under the dining table, to prevent any food that fell from the table from becoming trapped between the floorboards. These cloths are no longer used to catch crumbs, but nowadays they make marvelous runners or mats. They are also simple to make, and can be decorated with designs as complicated or as straightforward as you wish.

To make a crumb cloth, choose the heaviest duck canvas you can find; I used 10 ounce duck canvas. Stretch the canvas out on a large piece of board, a work table, the floor or even a hard surface in the garden, and pin it down with tacks around all the edges to keep it flat. Prime the canvas with a mixture of one part PVA glue – to make the canvas flexible – to three parts latex paint, in a pale color. Paint the mixture on with a small roller, allowing each coat to dry before applying the next; apply four or five coats altogether. The first two coats will be difficult to apply, as you have to work the mixture into the weave of the canvas, but thereafter it is a relatively quick process. Sand the surface lightly after the third coat. When you have finished priming,

apply two coats of latex background color using a roller. Leave to dry, then the cloth is ready to be stenciled.

My Moroccan design is a huge, but very simple stencil, and is quick and easy both to cut and to use. It consists of a large square with an eight-pointed star in each corner. The repeats could not be more straightforward: simply align the left-hand stars of the new repeat over the right-hand stars of the last one, and mask them out. This also keeps the design running straight.

Use latex paints to paint the design. Stipple the stars with a stencil brush and sponge the color on to the linking sections between the stars to give texture. Allow to dry.

Measure and mark a line an even distance in from the edge, and lightly score it with a table knife. Turn the edges of the canvas to the back of the cloth and stick down with strong adhesive.

Using a roller, apply at least two coats – ideally four or five – of acrylic, water-based varnish over the painted side of the cloth: the more coats you apply, the more durable the cloth will be. Acrylic varnish dries very quickly, and is ready for recoating after two hours. To avoid unnecessary brush-washing, wrap the paint brush you are using in a damp cloth between coats. When you have finished varnishing, you will need to leave the cloth to dry for two days before using it, otherwise it will not be water-resistant. The varnish should not affect the rug's flexibility.

Crumb cloths are quite sturdy when placed on floorboards; however, they will not take kindly to high heels, as the heels sink into the fabric and will crack the paint on the cloth.

OPPOSITE *The geometric design of the crumb cloth echoes the lines of the table and the window above, giving a pleasing visual structure to the room. The secret of keeping the pattern running straight lies in aligning the stars. I chose to use the same color for the square sides, but to vary the colors of the stars.*

RIGHT *Despite having four or five coats of acrylic varnish applied on top of the painted design, the fabric here (right) retains a fluid flexibility. The versatile crumb cloth provides a quick way to change the look of a room without the cost of redecorating. It also serves well as a rug for the garden, and can be extended in length to form a runner for the hall.*

The stencil motif supplied here is a greatly reduced version of the one I used for my crumb cloth, where the stars measured 6 inches across and the oblong strips measured 4 x 8 inches. To create a larger motif, enlarge it on a photocopier to 11 x 17 inches, then cut this sheet into six equal sections. Now enlarge each of these sections to 11 x 17 inches, and then stick them all together (see page 102 for full details).

I chose to color the stars in a random way, so giving added interest to the design. It is wise to plan the colorings before you start painting, because you will easily lose track of those colors masked out around your painting area.

When choosing new colors for a stencil design, I find it helpful to buy little tester pots of latex with which to experiment. These are an ideal way of trying out different colors without spending too much money, and the colors available now are so glorious that you will almost certainly find what you want without too much trial and error. An alternative method is to mix artist's acrylic colors into small amounts of white latex, adjusting the amount you add to achieve the effect you want. When you are satisfied, make sure you mix enough of your chosen color to finish the design.

## CANVAS PLACE MATS

Using the same technique as for crumb cloths, you can also make beautiful place mats from smaller pieces of canvas. Use just one of the stenciled squares to decorate place mats, or reduce the design in size and stencil several miniature squares. A stenciled place mat should be able to withstand the heat of all but the hottest of pots.

OPPOSITE *Do not be misled by the chalk-like quality of these stars: the softly colored paint will not rub off easily. Latex is a very durable paint, and some protective coats of terracotta sealer complete the tough finish.*

The big, bold star design from the Moroccan floorcloth can also be painted on terracotta floor tiles for a quick and cheap transformation in a room or terrace. Tiles can be decorated either loose or *in situ*, but remember to keep out tramping feet until the paint dries!

You could be forgiven for doubting that latex paint would be sufficiently durable for outdoor use; in fact, it adheres surprisingly well to this surface and has proved extremely hard-wearing. Use a stencil brush to paint the stenciled stars, varying your colors to add impact to the design. After allowing the paint to dry, finish off the decoration with two coats of terracotta sealer to prevent the paint from wearing away.

Once you have gained confidence on some single tiles, look around your garden to see what else you could transform. An uninspiring terrace or balcony could be given a new lease of life with a stenciled border of stars and oblongs, with perhaps a few extra stars scattered within the framed area. Complete the effect with some large plant pots decorated to match.

A mixture of cultures, using tiles decorated with the soft chalky colors of the Moroccan star design as a framework for a formal parterre garden, would look sensational. Use as many 'squares' of the design provided on page 77 as you need to divide your garden into separate areas for different flowers, herbs, shrubs, and so on, varying your colors for best effect. You may need to shorten the rectangles slightly so that each one can fit on to a tile. Plan your design carefully before you start stenciling, or you may end up with the wrong numbers of stars and rectangles. When all the stenciling is complete, seal the tiles with terracotta sealer, then start the task of laying out your jigsaw-like design.

If such a scheme seems too complicated, why not decorate some stepping stones? Flat stones or treetrunk rounds stenciled with Moroccan stars would make a colorful path across any lawn.

## STENCILED BUILDING BLOCKS

Children's wooden building blocks (see pages 78–9) can be personalized by stenciling simple designs on to their sides. Once reduced in scale, the Moroccan stars fitted neatly into the little squares, and the bright latex colors looked very cheerful. Seal the blocks with acrylic varnish to prevent the paint from chipping.

## WARNING

When decorating anything for children, whether it is toys, clothes or furniture, it is absolutely vital to ensure that the paint you use is non-toxic. Nowadays, most of the main brands available are safe and lead-free, but always check the paint labels carefully. If in doubt, contact the paint manufacturers direct.

# ZEBRA STRIPES

Inspired by a tapestry cushion that was decorated with a splendid stitched zebra, I wanted to design a zebra stencil. The tapestry zebra proved to be too fine and almost too realistic an image for an effective stencil, however, so I simplified the stripes drastically, and modeled the animal on a child's wooden toy. The end result is so charming that it is one of only a few designs that I think I could actually use to stencil a continuous border all around a room. You could design your own stencils of other animals to provide some contrast, but I decided that the border made more of an impact as a parade of toy zebras.

Make sure that the animal is big enough to be seen clearly, even when it is placed down by the baseboard; if they are too small and fiddly, the effect will not be so eye-catching. It is worthwhile making several practice zebras on heavy paper and placing them on the wall to check that the size and the space between each one is correct and consistent. Measure your room carefully and take the dimensions into consideration when you are deciding on the size and spacing of your animals, so that you do not have to stencil into a corner.

## ZEBRA PRINT CUSHIONS

Zebra stripes are wonderfully dramatic, even when they are separated from the zebra. To make a zebra print cushion, take a photocopy of the adapted zebra design reproduced on page 117,

OPPOSITE *This child-size chair is almost the same height as the high baseboard, which gives the illusion that the zebra border is farther up the wall than it really is. The bridges in this stencil are almost as wide as the windows, making for a dramatically stripy result.*

and then enlarge it several times, until it reaches the size of the cushion you want to make (see page 102 for advice on enlarging). Then, cut out a cushion back and front from white or off-white fabric, and using fabric paints, stencil the design on to the fabric. Painting the design before making up the cushion ensures that the decoration goes right to the edge of the cushion. Add a little brown paint to the black to warm the stripes, as black can look too stark. When the paint is dry, make up the cushion by placing the two sides together, with the painted sides facing each other, and stitching around three sides. Turn the cover the right-side out, insert the pillow form, and slipstich the opening.

For extra impact, I piped my cushions with black velvet piping. This was stitched to the painted side of one of the fabric squares, half an inch in from the edge; the other piece was then placed on top, so that the piping lay between the two sections of fabric and the cushion was stitched as above.

## ZEBRA PRINT THROW

Using a similar method to the cushions, a very effective zebra print throw can be made. For this, you will need a piece of linen of the required size, a piece of backing fabric the same size (the black velvet I chose for piping the cushions would look dramatic and be luxuriously soft), plus some cushion interlining the same size, to give the throw more body.

To make the print large enough for a throw, take two photocopies of the simplified zebra stripes on page 117. Place one copy underneath the other, so the two rectangles of design lie side by side, with one forming a mirror image of the other. Trace this mirror image on to your top

LEFT & OPPOSITE *You can also use this design to decorate clothing. I used a slightly smaller zebra to decorate my daughter's cotton T-shirt, stenciling the design all around the bottom. Use fabric paint for decorating clothing to ensure that the paint is not washed out. As with the cushion, add a touch of brown to the black to make the stripes a little warmer against the white fabric.*

copy, thus doubling the size of your original rectangle. Now enlarge this on to a sheet of paper 11 x 17 inches, following the instructions on page 102 until you reach the size you need. At this point you may want to add a few extra stripes to fill in any blank spaces. Transcribe your completed design on to stencil board; cut it out with a craft knife; then stipple it on to the linen, following the instructions on page 23.

When the paint is dry, place the backing fabric right-side up on a table, and lay the zebra print, wrong-side up, on top. Next place the interlining on the wrong side of the zebra print. Thus you have a sandwich in which the zebra print is the filling. Stitch through all three layers, half an inch in from the edge, leaving a small opening at one point. When you have finished stitching, turn the throw the right way out through this opening, and slipstitch the gap closed. Press the throw gently (particularly if you have a velvet backing), and top-stitch all around the edges.

# TARTAN

I have always been a great fan of conventional tartan with its warm and cosy feel, particularly in winter. However, I wanted a brighter, sunnier effect, so I used Mediterranean colors and adapted a traditional tartan. This cheerful design quickly brightens up a dull space, filling an open doorway with a blaze of color, and turning a white and rather clinical laundry room (see page 88) into a cheery place where one would be almost pleased to have to go to sort the washing.

## MAKING TWO-STAGE STENCILS

Designs such as tartans often require two-stage stencils. Not to be confused with masking stencils, a two-stage stencil is, in fact, two separate stencils that can be used quite happily on their own, one design being overlaid by a different one. In this case, the second stencil conveniently masks out the first, but it is not necessarily so with all two-stage stencils. For this tartan design, I made one stencil for the green, and another for the yellow which masked out the green (see page 125).

Cut the stencils on the largest piece of board you can find, repeating the design to cover the entire sheet, so that you can spray as large an area as possible at one time. Start at the top of the fabric if you are stenciling a curtain, and work your way along the top edge, which you can use as a straight line for lining up the whole pattern. Then go back to where you started and work your way down one side edge. Finally, fill in the right angle. If your planned design is for a wall, start at the bottom and work up one side edge. Rather than confusing yourself by

having to swap cans of paint every two minutes, you can do a number of repeats with your first stencil in one color, before going back and following up with the second stencil and second color. Always mark the top of both stencils so that you use them the same way up, and be careful when lining up the second stencil: one slip could set all the second-color repeats out of alignment with the first.

Measuring is important when stenciling pattern repeats, but on my tartan design the edges are slightly rounded and the squares slightly uneven, so there is room to juggle if necessary. If the lines were exactly straight, there would be no room to maneuver a slightly smaller, or larger, square to fit an awkward space. The slightly rounded shapes also give a softer, more informal effect.

Unless you are in the habit of constantly washing your curtains, they can be stenciled perfectly acceptably with spray paints, which are, moreover, much easier and quicker to use on a large scale than fabric paints. If you seam and hem the curtains before you decorate them, you can stencil over the joins in the fabric lengths, which makes for a much neater finish. Beware, though: if the curtains are at this stage, there is no room for mistakes. Similarly, do not be tempted to slacken off the cords in the pleating tape of an existing pair of curtains, because you will never get the fabric to lie sufficiently smooth and flat for successful stenciling.

When decorating walls, sooner or later you will come across an electricity socket. To deal with this, leave the area of one stencil blank

LEFT *This double doorway leading into a kitchen has been given a bright, summery look with this tartan curtain in a Provençal-style blend of blue and yellow. I scaled down the design and reduced the size of the tartan squares for this from 14 inches to 9 inches.*

LEFT & OPPOSITE *Designs like tartans, based on two patterns, require two-stage stencils (see page 86), where one stencil is overlaid by another. For this tartan, the second, yellow stencil, conveniently masks the design of the green stencil, although this is not always the case with two-stage stencils.*

*• When decorating a wall, you may find sockets in the way. Leave blank a space the size of one stencil around the socket and finish stenciling. Then come back to the blank area, and cut your stencil to fit around the socket. To be safe, spray a copy of the stencil before you destroy the original.*

89

RIGHT *Stenciling before sticking down allows you to extend a stenciled pattern right into a corner, an effect that is impossible to achieve when stenciling directly on to a surface.*

OPPOSITE *Stenciled paper can also be used to cover books, both to protect them and to brighten them up.*

around the socket, and carry on stenciling the rest of the wall. After you have finished, come back to the blank area, and cut your stencil to fit the socket. As you will have finished the rest of the room, and have no further use for the stencil, you can ruin it with impunity; but, just to be safe, spray a copy of the stencil before you destroy the original.

Tartan is a very versatile design, with endless opportunities for variation. The pattern I used for the wall and curtains had a large, square grid with narrow borders, but for smaller-scale work, such as paper, I adapted the design to produce borders of varying thicknesses.

## STENCILING PAPER

When stenciling decorative paper for lining chests of drawers and trunks, use the heaviest lining paper you can find.

The two-stage stencil (see page 125) looks as if it might take forever to cut, but, because the design is so simple, it is in fact not that time-consuming. Firstly, cut out all the right-hand edges of all the squares on the first stencil, beveling the edges (see page 102). Now, turn the board through 90 degrees, and again cut all the right-hand edges. Repeat the turning and cutting until all the sides are complete, and all the squares drop out very satisfyingly. Now repeat the whole process for the second stencil. To ensure that the design is printed straight, make the paper stencils half an inch wider than the paper itself, with registration marks at each end to mark the width of the paper. Before stenciling, always line up the registration marks with the paper edges.

Unroll the paper on a table, and position your first stencil. Place protective newspaper all around the stencil. Spray with your first color,

then remove the stencil and replace it with the second one, checking the registration marks. Spray with your second color. Repeat this process all down the roll of paper, moving the stencil down the table as you go. As spray paints dry so quickly, you can replace each stencil almost immediately, and can roll up the painted paper very quickly.

Cut the printed paper exactly to size and stick it down with wallpaper paste; once wet with the paste, it will fit happily into the tightest of corners.

# MOSAIC

Mosaics really have stood the test of time: patterns laid hundreds, if not thousands, of years ago still exist today, and continue to look beautiful. The careful placing of small stones or tiles on to a cement bed is, however, extremely time-consuming and so can be prohibitively expensive, which makes a stenciled mosaic a much cheaper and more adaptable option. It is also much easier to execute than it looks.

## STENCILING A FLOOR MOSAIC

The stencil design is made up of two motifs – a corner piece and a repeating straight section to form the sides. Make your stencils from the templates provided on page 127, following the instructions on pages 102–105. The repeat stencil will be positioned by the horizontal line you mark across the middle of the stencil board. The corner stencil needs two positioning lines, which are marked on the template itself; make sure you copy these lines on to your stencil, as these are vital for positioning your border. As with the tartan design, it is also most important that the top of the stencil is marked. I considered the top to be the edge placed nearest to the wall.

As the mosaic squares are slightly irregular in shape, and have rounded edges, they are a delight to cut. It does not matter too much if your hand slips a little with the knife, and some stones end up uneven.

Sand and fill your floor as required to achieve a smooth finish. I first sealed my floor with two coats of multipurpose PVA glue, diluted 1 : 5 with water and applied with a small paint roller. I then painted the floor with two coats of cream latex,

in between which I lightly sanded the floor. When the latex was completely dry, I applied at least two coats of acrylic varnish with a roller. This protects the paint and allows you to walk on it without marking it.

Measure the room thoroughly and be aware of any problem areas, such as recesses and fireplaces, etc. Decide where your mosaic border will be positioned, and mark the first two lines of the design on the floor with a water-soluble pencil (lines 1 and 2 in the diagram). These will be the lines on which you center your border.

Align the positioning lines of the corner piece with lines 1 and 2 on your floor; this starting point is corner A on the diagram. Stencil the pattern, then position the repeat pattern to the right of the corner piece, placing it where you think it should go by eye, and then slipping it back a bit along the line to bring into view the last small mosaic square that you have just painted (if you are using aerosols, this will not smudge it). Now move the stencil forward again

OPPOSITE *You should not need registration marks on your stencils for the pattern repeats with this mosaic border because the lines marked on the stencil board and the floor should keep your design running straight.*

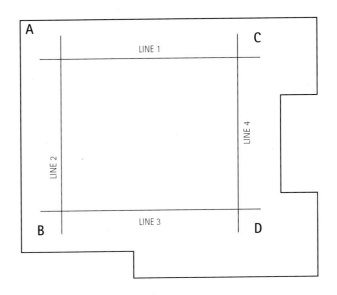

by about quarter of an inch, or the distance between the mosaic squares. The board should now be in the right place for you to stencil your first repeat. Now work gradually outwards along the lines, stenciling one or two repeats on line 1, then doing the same on line 2, allowing the paint time to dry thoroughly, until you approach corners B and C. As you work, make sure the horizontal line on your repeat stencil matches up with your floor lines, in order to keep the design running straight. You will eventually obscure the line on your board with paint, so keep drawing it in.

Do not worry too much about accurate or precise positioning: as the laying of true mosaics is, by its very nature, a slightly imprecise business, it does not matter if your repeats vary slightly; in fact, any slight variation is almost certain to go unnoticed.

Unless you have been lucky, you will not reach corners B and C at the end of a full repeat, so you need to decide before you get there whether you want to stop early and have a slightly wider-than-planned gap between your design and the wall, or whether to paint one more repeat and have a slighter narrower gap. You need to be flexible about the exact position of these corners, but, having made the decision about how many repeats you want to use, you will now be able to mark in line 3 and then line 4.

Continue around the room, stenciling one or two repeats on one side before going to the other and doing the same. It is helpful to keep count of the straight repeats, to ensure that lines 1 and 3 and lines 2 and 4 contain equal numbers.

Aim to finish at the least important part of the room, where any adjustments you might have to make will not be too noticeable. As real mosaic squares are rarely all the same size, it does not matter if you have to mask out some of your painted squares to get everything to fit.

When the border is finished and the paint has dried, apply two coats of acrylic varnish so that your mosaic is protected from dirt and wear.

### STENCILING A CURTAIN BORDER

The mosaic design is also suitable for curtains. I stenciled it on to a fine muslin curtain, and it looks marvelous: the fluid lines of the design echo the flowing lines of the fabric. It is simple to do, because it is only a straight run of a simple pattern repeat running along the bottom of the material. If you are painting on to an already hemmed curtain made of muslin or other thin fabric, it is advisable to undo the hem before stenciling in case the two layers of fabric on the hem move against each other and smudge the design. You can sew up the hem when the paint is dry. If you are making the curtain yourself, wait to hem it until after the stenciling is complete.

For this design I used pale cream fabric paints which looked very subtle, but the design would look equally stunning in a vibrant pink or green.

BELOW *Spray paints seep into fabric, producing a quasi-stained effect, whereas fabric paints, stippled on, create a slightly raised texture on the fabric that is more akin to the raised, uneven surface of authentic mosaic stones.*

# CURLICUES

After revamping a party dress for my daughter Lois, by stenciling a red curlicue around the hem, it occurred to me that a simple wavy line could be put to other uses.

## PAINTING TWO-COLOR WALLS

A curlicue separating the areas of a wall painted in two different colors looks attractive, and is much less formal than the straight line of a dado. It is also easier to paint than a straight line.

Matching where the two colors meet with the curlicue stencil is not difficult. First, measure up from the floor and mark the desired height for the stencil. Paint the top half of the wall in your first latex color, extending the paint by about 2 inches below the marked line. To create the wavy dividing line, first make up the curlicue stencil (see pages 6-7) and then spray a series of adjacent copies of it on to a new, wide piece of stencil board. Then, following the main curves of the design, cut this board so that the bottom edge forms a 'wave' shape.

It is sensible to start work from the middle of the wall. Tape the wave template/mask to the wall so it lies between the marked line and the bottom of the first paint color, then use your second latex color to paint the wall from this point down to the ground or baseboard. Remove the template to reveal a wavy line separating the two colors. Continue around the room. At the corners, you may like to cut the template so as to continue the wave around onto the adjoining wall.

Once the latex paint on the walls is dry, position the curlicue stencil along the top side

of the wavy line, use newspaper to mask the surrounding wall and cover the floor, and then spray with your chosen color.

## CHILDREN'S PARTY CLOTHES

Children quickly tire of their party clothes, so stenciling a design on to them to match new accessories can quickly rejuvenate both the outfit and the child's interest in it. I stenciled a wavy line along the bottom of Lois's dress, and one along the frilly collar, in a color to match her shoes and hair ribbon. You can use spray paint for this decoration, as party dresses are not often used, but fabric paints will last longer and be more suitable for washing. Although they used to be available in only a few, mostly bright, colors, the range of fabric paints, including metallic and neon shades, is now extensive.

OPPOSITE *Mustard yellow meets purple, with a neat curlicue to separate the two colors. If you find that you do have to work into a corner, the stencil is so quick and easy to make that you can simply take a copy of it, cut it out and use that copy to bend into the corner.*

99

# WORKING WITH STENCILS

Read the following pages
to learn the basic techniques
for stenciling, then practise
on anything you can find –
paper, fabric, a wooden
shed, a brick wall – to gain
confidence. This practising
can be just as much fun
as painting the final design.
Be prepared to experiment
with the images provided
and have fun designing
your own.

# MAKING A STENCIL

You will find images to use for making stencils throughout this book. After you have chosen one, you can either trace it to make a stencil of the same size, or take it to a photocopying shop and have it reproduced at whatever size you want. It is worth taking time to plan your stencil to fit your chosen location: there is nothing more infuriating than finding that the stencil you have taken such care to prepare is, in fact, just that little bit too big or too small for the space you wish to decorate.

If you want to create a really large stencil, such as the greyhound on page 71, first enlarge your design on a photocopier to fit on to 11 x 17 inch paper. Cut the enlarged image into six and then enlarge each of these sections to fit on to the same size paper. When you fit these six sections together, you will have a greatly enlarged image of your motif. The edges of images can become a little fuzzy when they are blown up, so it is worth drawing over them to sharpen them up a bit. On very big enlargements, you might need to alter the design slightly, so that it all balances. If I was magnifying the pea pod on page 19, for example, I would add more, smaller peas to the pod instead of having three large peas.

If you have enlarged or reduced a stencil template, check that the bridges of the stencil are going to be firm enough to hold the stencil together once it is cut – they should not be narrower than about an eighth of an inch. Bridges add strength to the stencil and help to add definition and interest to the design.

*OPPOSITE For a beveled edge, which helps to stop the paint from seeping under the stencil board, keep your craft knife at an angle of roughly 45 degrees, with the blade innermost as you cut.*

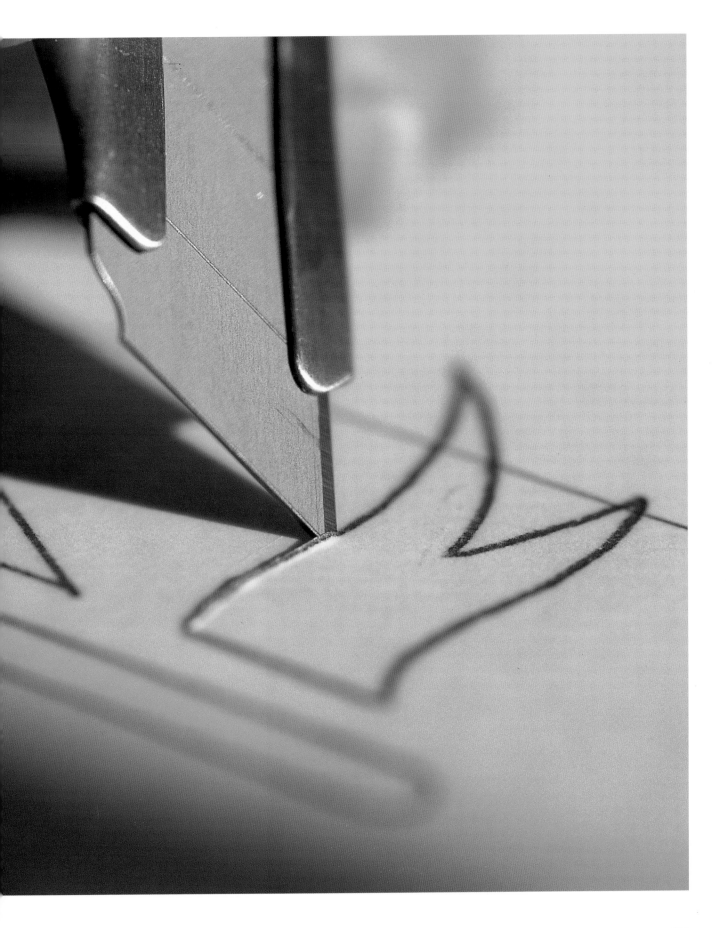

RIGHT *Using the center marks for alignment, place your design on top of some carbon paper, and stick both in position on the stencil board.*

FAR RIGHT *Use a crayon or ballpoint pen to distinguish the new lines as you transfer the design.*

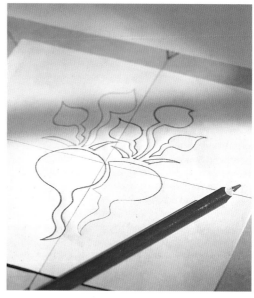

### TRACING A DESIGN

Take your blank stencil board, which should be about twice the size of your design. Draw two diagonals across it, to find its center, and add horizontal and vertical lines through the middle. Roughly cut around the outside of your design. Stick it on to the non-carbon side of a piece of carbon paper using spray adhesive, and then stick the whole thing, carbon side down, on to the center of your stencil board, using your center marks for guidance.

Trace over the image, including the bridges. When you have finished, remove the image and carbon paper. Clarify the carbon lines by running over them again with a colored pencil or a ballpoint pen.

If you are not quite happy with your design, or you would like to make adaptations, this is the stage at which to alter it. If you have quite a complicated design, you may want to clarify which of your lines mark the bridges, and which the windows, by shading in the windows. You can then tell at a glance which pieces are to be cut out.

### CUTTING A STENCIL

With your stencil card placed squarely on your cutting board, start to cut out your design with your craft knife. Always keep your free hand above the blade, so that you will not cut yourself. Starting in the middle of your design and working outwards, push the knife through the board, and then ease the pressure slightly as you draw the knife towards you.

Keep your knife at an angle of roughly 45 degrees inward in order to achieve a beveled edge. Cut out the smaller windows first, starting at the right-hand side of each shape (or left-hand side if you are left-handed), and moving the board rather than the knife when the design changes direction. Then turn your board around, through 180 degrees, and cut out the rest of each shape; if you try to cut both sides at the same time, you will have problems with beveling.

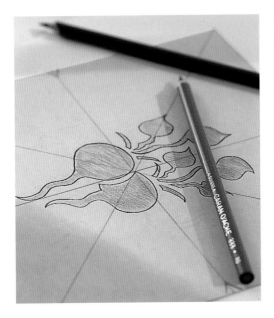

FAR LEFT *Color in the areas of the stencil to be cut out, so you do not cut the bridges by mistake.*

LEFT *Start cutting at the right-hand side of each shape (or left-hand for left-handers), moving the stencil board, not the knife, when you change direction.*

You can use a ruler for straight lines, but I tend not to, as I find that, unless I am cutting a geometric design, dead straight lines can look too clinical. Try to take your knife out as few times as possible to avoid tiny hiccups in your lines.

If you cut through a bridge by mistake, or one breaks at any point, finish the cut you have started. Then take two small pieces of masking tape. Stick one over the break, turn the board over and then stick the second on the back, pressing the edges of the pieces of tape together. Turn the board over again, and re-cut the affected edges with a beveled edge. Remove the cut pieces.

STENCIL PAPER

Take care when you are cutting images out of stencil paper; it is not a very forgiving medium, and it is easy to make mistakes. However, you may well find that its low cost and the usefulness of its transparency outweigh any handling difficulties.

ACETATE

Heat pens are the best tools for cutting acetate. Draw your design on to the acetate with a very fine permanent marker, then, resting the acetate on glass (to protect your work surface), trace your design with the heat pen. Keep the heat pen upright, and keep it moving: if you are distracted, or stop, you risk burning a hole in the acetate. Confidence is important when you are cutting your stencil because you cannot rectify a mistake on acetate.

REGISTRATION MARKS

For a repeating pattern, you will need to cut tiny registration marks in your stencil board, one on the left and one on the right exactly equidistant from the design and at the same height. For example, if your left-hand hole is half an inch from the start of the design and 1 inch from the top of the stencil, then your right-hand hole must be half an inch from the end of the design, and 1 inch from the top of the stencil (see picture on page 106).

# APPLYING COLOR

RIGHT *Registration marks at the top and bottom, as well as at the sides, are useful for aligning vertically repeating patterns.*

FAR RIGHT *Use masking tape to hold down the protective paper and also to mask the area of the stencil not being painted.*

When you have cut your stencil, take some time to practise stenciling before decorating your chosen surface. Rolls of heavy paper provide an excellent surface to practise on, being highly absorbent and pleasingly inexpensive.

I stencil almost exclusively with spray paint, and would recommend using it for a number of reasons: it dries almost immediately; it creates a lovely texture; it is incredibly durable, which makes it suitable for outdoors as well as indoors; and it is quick and easy to use.

Before you begin to use your stencil, it is a good idea to create a duplicate stencil by spraying a copy of the newly cut board on to a clean stencil board. With this, you can cut a fresh version if the original stencil clogs or breaks.

## PREPARING SURFACES

When you have finished practising, you can prepare the surface to be stenciled, which means making sure that it is clean, dry and free from dust. Brick and terracotta need to be sealed, inside (for pots) and out, to stop the paint from soaking in: paint on a coat of water-based varnish or an equal mixture of spirit-based stain and denatured alcohol. A slightly crumbly surface, sealed with a suitable stabilizer, produces a mottled effect.

## POSITIONING

With all the windows open, spray the reverse of your stencil with spray adhesive, and stick it firmly on to the surface. You can position it either by eye, or more precisely using a ruler, plumbline and spirit level. If you are stenciling a vertical or rounded surface, or brickwork, secure the stencil with pieces of masking tape as well as adhesive. Protect the area surrounding your stencil with brown paper or newspaper, taped in place, and protect the floor with drop cloths.

## SPRAYING PAINT

Shake the can of spray paint vigorously for up to

106

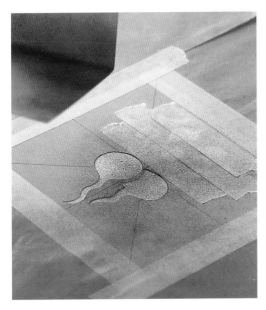

FAR LEFT *Spray on the color for the first part of the motif, using the baffle to deflect the force of the spray paint.*

LEFT *Uncover the masked area, then cover the painted area with masking tape and spray on the second color.*

a minute (longer if the weather is cold) and, wearing a protective face mask, give one or two bursts of paint on to a piece of scrap paper, to check that the paint is flowing smoothly and that you have picked up the right color. Hold the spray can about 10 inches from the stencil, then take the baffle in your other hand and hold it roughly halfway between the can and the stencil. Spray in short bursts, of less than a second, directed at the top of the baffle, and

moving the can away from you. The baffle takes the first, strong burst of paint, and the trailing-off goes on to the stencil. This will take a bit of practice to get right. Try to spray two or three light coats of paint rather than one heavy coat, as the heavier the spray, the more likely the paint is to seep under the stencil. You could also try to vary the amount of spray as you paint, to achieve different effects. Shake the can occasionally to stop the nozzle from getting clogged with paint.

As you are effectively spraying the baffle and not the stencil, the baffle can become drenched with paint. If you are not careful, this can drip on to your stencil. To avoid this, cut off bits of the baffle as they become drenched. If you do drip paint from the baffle, or use so much paint that it seeps under the stencil; or, indeed, if the spray has gone beyond your protective sheeting, dip a cotton swab into cellulose thinners, and clean up the mistake as best you can.

When you become more experienced, you can use the baffle to vary the shading across a motif. Spray your stencil lightly all over, then move the baffle to protect most of the design and spray again, so that you get a little extra paint on just one edge. If you want to use two colors, the baffle can guard areas that you want to keep clean for the second color.

For simple two-color designs, use masking tape to shield the different areas of the stencil (see photographs above).

# MASKING STENCILS

*If you want to use several colors in a design, but feel that they will end up muddied using the baffle alone, then you may decide to mask out parts of your stencil. For simple designs that are not being used repeatedly, the easiest thing is to use masking tape to cover up parts of the stencil. For more complex stencils, or repeating patterns, an easier way around the problem is to make a masking stencil.*

*To do this, stick your original stencil down on to stencil board with spray adhesive, and lightly stencil the image on to the second card. Remove the original stencil. Decide what colors you want the different areas of your final image to be. On the freshly stenciled board, draw a line around all the areas to be stenciled in your first color to make them into one block. Repeat this process for each color. To remind you of the color of an individual block, draw around each using colored pens in an appropriate shade.*

*I have outlined three blocks on my sailing boat stencil: a blue block consisting of the mast and the hull, a yellow block for the foresail and the pennant, and a red block for the mainsail.*

*When you have marked all the colors, cut out each block (following the colored lines) with a craft knife in the same way as you cut the original stencil (see page 102). Each block forms a part of the masking stencil. There is no limit to the number of colors you can use, but the greater the number, the smaller (and more fiddly) the pieces of the masking stencil will be.*

*Masking stencils are very easy to use, but it is advisable to practise on heavy paper before finally stenciling your designated space. Stick down the original stencil; then stick the corresponding pieces of the masking stencil over it, leaving one of the color areas uncovered. Spray the uncovered area in your chosen color.*

# ADJUSTING STENCILS

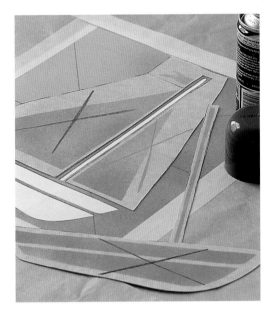

FAR LEFT *Use the masking stencil pieces to cover those areas that are not going to be painted first.*

LEFT *Spray on your first color, using the baffle. Within seconds, you can cover up the painted area with its piece of the masking stencil and uncover another.*

Leaving just a few seconds for the paint to dry, cover this area with its masking piece (as spray paint dries so quickly, the surface will not be damaged by being covered). Uncover another area of color, and spray this in the appropriate color. Continue in this way until you have finished painting the stencil. Then remove all the masking pieces to reveal the final design.

The process may sound complicated, but in fact it is very easy, and each masking stencil piece can be used repeatedly.

## REPEATING STENCILS

When you are using repeats of the same stencil, measure the space to be decorated and work out how many repeats you will need. Careful calculations before you cut your stencil should ensure that the repeats will fit exactly into the space. If you run into a problem, you can adjust your stencil by masking out what you do not need, or cut a new piece by adapting your design to fit in the gap. Try to juggle things, increasing or decreasing the space between repeats, so that everything fits.

Transparent stencil paper and acetate make for easy repositioning when you use repeated designs for a border; with opaque stencil board, it is slightly more complicated. If your stencil has repeated images within it, such as the bubbles motif (see page 39), you can align your stencil over the painted images, masking these with tape as you spray the repositioned stencil, so that they do not become too heavily painted. If your stencil has no repeated images in it, you can make a tiny dot in soft pencil in the right-hand registration mark when you paint, so that when you reposition your stencil, you can align the left-hand hole over the pencil dot.

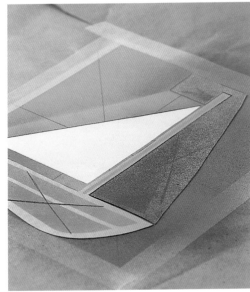

FAR LEFT *Spray on the second block of color – which has two parts.*

LEFT *Finally, spray in the third color to complete the design.*

OPPOSITE *The finished stencil, with all the masking pieces removed.*

## CORNERS

*If you need to turn a right-angled corner on a small, repeating design, such as around a tray, you can miter the corner by covering the second half of the stencil with masking tape, making an angle of 45 degrees across the design. When you have finished painting the stencil up to the masking tape, remove the stencil, take off the tape and mask the first half of the stencil, again at 45 degrees. Repositioning the newly masked stencil at right angles to your last piece of stenciling will give you a corner as neatly mitered as a picture frame. If you are copying one of the images at the end of this book, you will find that the border motifs are supplied with helpful corner sections.*

*Try to avoid spraying into the corners of a room, for example with borders; with careful forward planning, you should be able to get your stencil to finish about 2 inches from the corner, starting again 2 inches out. If this fails, do not be tempted to bend your stencil into the corner and spray through it: the stencil will not stick right into the corner, and paint will seep through leaving you with a blurred image.*

*If you absolutely must stencil into a corner, put a 1 inch wide strip of masking tape into the corner, so you have half an inch on each side of the corner, gently bend your stencil without creasing it, and then spray – nobody will notice a tiny gap in the design.*

## ADAPTING STENCILS

*Stencils can be adapted for different locations. There are pea pods in the vegetable trug stencil on one of my trays (see page 18), for example, and I have used just the peas on a little bowl. In some instances, you can mask out the parts of the stencil that you do not want, but sometimes the whole stencil can be the wrong shape for the new location. The trug stencil, however well masked, was far too big to fit snugly into the bowl. To adapt the stencil, take a copy of the whole design, and recut just the area that you want.*

*Another example of adapting a stencil is the climbing squashes (see pages 25–7). Having cut a fairly complicated stencil, I was loathe to cut another to add variety to the design. Instead I cut one new piece of stem, and achieved the rest with crafty masking.*

# ADDITIONAL TECHNIQUES

As an alternative to using spray paint, you can use stencil brushes, sponges and rollers. Each of these produces a different paint effect, ranging from mottled to smooth. Experiment to discover which effect you prefer.

## STENCIL BRUSH

Stencil brushes and paint are much easier to control than spray paints. They require much less masking out or cutting of masking stencils. Use stencil paints, or try artist's acrylic paints diluted with water to the consistency of heavy cream. Even latex paint is suitable; in fact, anything can be used as long as it is quick-drying so that there is no danger of smudging your newly painted design.

To load a stencil brush (which should always be used dry), pour a small amount of paint into a saucer. Take your brush and swish the end of it around in the paint, getting an even coating on its tip, and then wipe off the excess on a paper towel. Alternatively, load the brush with color from a stencil crayon, or rub some paint from the crayon on to a piece of stencil board, before loading your brush by dabbing and swirling it in the color. The brush should still look fairly dry.

Holding your brush upright, dab it on to the secured stencil, moving all over the stencil in a random manner, to achieve an irregular effect, and gradually work up your design.

Get into a rhythm as you work, keeping your wrist loose as you bounce the upright brush up and down on the stencil. Unless you want muddy colors, always change your stencil brush between colors.

When shading your design, start in the middle and radiate outwards, dabbing on the color as you prefer. Masking out is not often necessary, unless you are using a very small stencil, in which case a piece of masking tape will do the job.

As soon as you have finished using your brushes, put them in a glass jar with warm soapy water, and swish them around in the water to clean off the paint. Then shake the brushes to remove the excess water before leaving them in a warm place to dry.

## NET

To create a softly pitted texture (see opposite), place a piece of fine mesh or net on the surface to be decorated. Stick the stencil in position in the usual way, and spray the paint through the stencil and the net/mesh.

## SPONGE

Using a sponge to apply the color creates a distinctive texture that varies depending on the type of sponge you use. Natural sponges produce a subtle, mottled look, whereas synthetic sponges give a more even, pitted finish. Load the sponge with as little paint as possible to avoid a messy effect.

## PAINT ROLLER

Using a small paint roller produces a smooth finish with no brushmarks at all. To load the roller, roll it back and forth in a tray of paint, taking care not to overload it. Then roll the paint roller over the stencil to apply the color.

## SPRAY EFFECTS

Various metallic sprays can give a good finish to some designs – even the bright, Christmassy golds, if used sparingly. Hold the baffle in one hand to block most of the paint, and spray the tips and edges of your design very lightly. Alternatively, use a gold pen to highlight the edges.

For a completely matt effect, you can use a spray primer for your stenciling, which has a dusty, *chalky finish. To prevent it from being rubbed off, spray your work with artist's fixative, or unperfumed hair spray.*

## STORING STENCILS

*Leave your stencils flat to dry thoroughly and scrape away any brush hairs or fabric fibers before storing them. Keep all the pieces of the original and masking stencils together. Place the stencils on top of each other, and keep them as flat and dry as possible. Stencils will eventually become clogged with paint – the smaller the design, the quicker this will happen – though this can add to the character of the design. Stencils used with spray paints tend to last longer than those used with stencil paints, as the layers of paint from a can are thinner than those from a brush. When your stencil needs replacing, simply cut a new one using your duplicate stencil (see page 106).*

SPRAY PAINT WITH SHADING EFFECT

SPONGING

SPRAYING THROUGH NET

STIPPLING THROUGH MESH

# INDEX

## INDEX *(continued)*

## SUPPLIERS

**THE CHESHIRE CAT**

538 - 3RD STREET

CANMORE, ALBERTA

CANADA T1W 2J4

Phone: 403-678-3247

**DESIGNER STENCILS**

c/o The Stencil Shoppe Inc.

3634 Silverside Road

Wilmington, Delaware

USA 19810

Phone: 1-800-822-7836

Fax: 302-477-0170

Web: http://www.designerstencils. com

**L.A.STENCILWORKS**

16115 Vanowen St.

Van Nuys, California

USA 91406

Phone: 818-989-0262

Fax: 818-989-0405

Website: http://www.lastencil.com

**RED LION STENCILS**

1232 First NH Turnpike

Northwood, New Hampshire

USA 03261

Phone & Fax: 603-942-8949

**ROYAL DESIGN STUDIO**

386 East 8th St. Suite 209-188

Chula Vista, California

USA 91910

Phone: 1-800-747-9767

**THE SIMS COLLECTION**

Sims Design

24 Tower Cres

Barrie, Ontario

Canada L4N 2V2

Phone: 705-725-0152

Fax: 705-725-8637

**THE STENCIL ARTISANS LEAGUE, INC.**

10521 St. Charles Rock Road, Suite One

St. Ann, Missouri

USA 63074

Phone: 314-429-3459

Website: http://www.sali.org

**STENCIL EMPORIUM**

23994 Aliso Creek Road

Laguna Niguel, California

USA 92677

Phone: 714-448-8380

Fax: 714-448-7110

**STENCILS BY NANCY**

15206 Walters Road

Houston, Texas

USA 77068

Phone: 281-893-2227

Fax: 281-893-6733

# STENCIL MOTIFS

*Enlarge this design to the required size for the zebra cushion (see pages 83–5). For the throw, take two copies of the design, and place them side by side to create a mirror image (see page 85), then enlarge as necessary.*

This symmetrically designed leaf motif decorates the coir floor mat (see pages 62-3).

The final touch to the leaf design surrounding a window is provided by this wispy flourish (see pages 60-1).

For a sleepy companion rather than an alert guard dog (see page 71) choose this stencil.

Enlarged to lifesize, these gardening tools can make excellent trompe l'oeil decoration (see page 35).

*The vegetable trug design (see page 18) can be varied with the addition of other garden produce.*

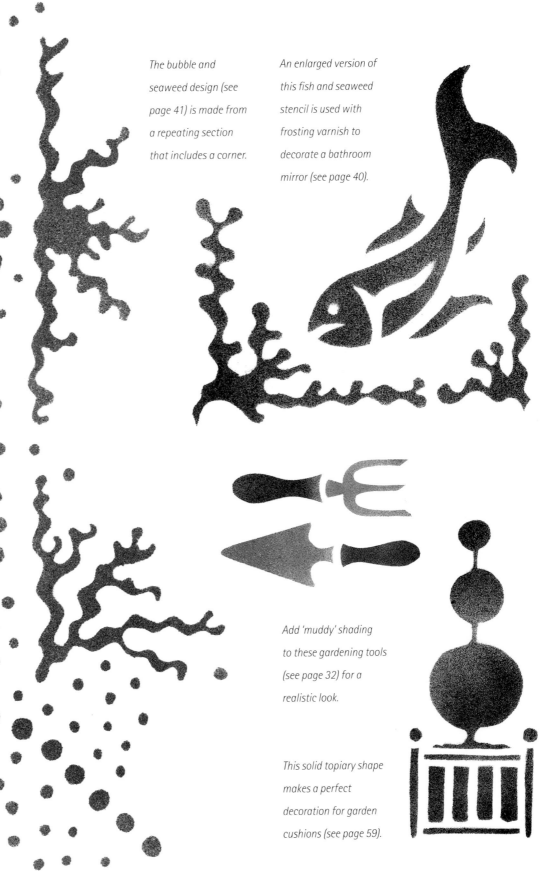

The bubble and seaweed design (see page 41) is made from a repeating section that includes a corner.

An enlarged version of this fish and seaweed stencil is used with frosting varnish to decorate a bathroom mirror (see page 40).

Add 'muddy' shading to these gardening tools (see page 32) for a realistic look.

This solid topiary shape makes a perfect decoration for garden cushions (see page 59).

This two-part stencil produces the tartan design on the lining paper (see pages 90–1). For the first stencil, cut out all the black squares; for the second, cut out all the grey areas.